PRAYERS
AT EASTERTIME

Written by Pamela Kennedy
Illustrated by Stephanie McFetridge Britt

IDEALS CHILDREN'S BOOKS
Nashville, Tennessee

Copyright © 1989 by Ideals Publishing Corporation
All rights reserved.
Printed and bound in the United States of America.
Published by Ideals Publishing Corporation
Nelson Place at Elm Hill Pike
Nashville, Tennessee

ISBN 0-8249-8422-6

Spring is the time
for flying kites
and jumping rope,
for playing baseball
and shooting marbles.

Did you play games
when you were little, Jesus?
If you were here,
I'd let you share my toys.

*Jesus said, "Let the little children
come to me."*

Matthew 19:14

**T**hank you
for the sounds
of spring, dear God—
the bubbling streams
and chirping birds,
the chattering chipmunks
and croaking frogs.

You make everything
sound so glad!

See! The winter is past;
the rains are over and gone.
Flowers appear on the earth;
the season of singing has come.

Song of Solomon 2:11-12

 planted some seeds
in my garden today, God.
I covered them with dirt
and I watered them
with my sprinkling can.

But that's all I can do.
Please send the rain
and let the sun shine
so my seeds will grow.

I planted the seed . . . but God made it grow.

1 Corinthians 3:6

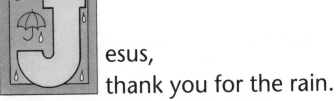

Jesus,
thank you for the rain.
It makes rivers for my boats
and puddles for my boots
and squishy mud for pies.

I like to hear
the drippy, droppy rain song
in the night.

I will send you rain in its season.

Leviticus 26:4

 was having
so much fun today,
Jesus, that I forgot to come
when Mama called.

And I wore my muddy boots
into the house.
I think I need to say,
"I'm sorry and I'll do better."

*The Lord is Lord of all
and richly blesses all who call on him.*

Romans 10:12

ometimes
it's hard to wait
for the rain to stop,
for the seeds to grow,
and for summer
to finally come.

Do you ever get tired
of waiting, Jesus?
Maybe if we wait together,
it won't seem so long.

*Be still before the Lord
and wait patiently for him.*

Psalm 37:7

ear Jesus,
I feel sick today.
My head hurts
and my nose is stuffy.

Mama says it's a cold,
but I feel hot.
Please help me feel better,
so I can go out and play.

O Lord, my God, I called to you for help
and you healed me.

Psalm 30:2

esus, guess what
I found today?
They're gray and soft,
just like kittens,
but they grow on a stick.

Daddy says they're pussywillows,
and that means spring is here.
Thank you for filling the world
with pretty things!

The earth is the Lord's and
everything in it.

Psalm 24:1

ometimes
I'm scared
when there's a storm.
The wind blows so hard
that the trees creak.
The lightning flashes
and the thunder booms so loudly
that my window rattles.

Then I remember
that you are stronger
than the storm, God,
and it helps me
not to be afraid.

I will fear no evil for you are with me.

Psalm 23:4

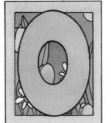n Easter Day
we go to church.
I love to smell the flowers
and hear the songs.

But the best part is to know
that you are still alive, Jesus,
and to remember
that you love even me.

We love because he first loved us.

1 John 4:19